Pawpaw is My Favorite Flavor

Written by Kaitlin Kulich

Illustrated by Laura Dobrota

ISBN: 978-0-692-17256-8

Monday Creek Publishing LLC
mondaycreekpublishing.com

To my Grandpas, Curt Schlarb and Bill Kulich, Sr.
~Kaitlin Kulich

To my son Luca, whose bright smiles were the inspiration behind Henry's character. May you always keep smiling!
~ Laura Dobrota

Finally, it was Saturday. The day Henry had been waiting for all week. He was going to visit his Grandpa in Athens, Ohio. Henry loved visiting his Grandpa because every visit, his Grandpa would teach him something new or take him on an exciting adventure on his farm.

As his mom drove down the highway to Grandpa's house, Henry gazed out the window at the beautiful Appalachian Mountains wondering what Grandpa had planned for them to do.

Once they arrived at Grandpa's farm, Henry jumped out of the car, ran over to Grandpa and gave him a big hug. "What are we going to do today Grandpa?" asked Henry. "Let's take a walk, and I'll show you," said Grandpa. "I think you will really like what I have planned!"

So Henry and Grandpa waved goodbye to Henry's mom and set off down a path on the farm. It was September, and the trees across the farm had begun to change into their fall colors.

As Henry and Grandpa walked further down the path, they came across a tree that looked different than all the others. It was much shorter than the other trees and had big green fruit hanging from its branches.

"What kind of tree is this Grandpa?" asked Henry.

This is a pawpaw tree!" explained Grandpa. "We are going to pick the fruit and make pawpaw ice cream today!"

"Are you sure it tastes good?" asked Henry.

Of course, I'm sure!" Grandpa said. "Pawpaw is my favorite flavor!"

While reaching for a pawpaw, a butterfly with black and white stripes flew by Henry's face. "That butterfly looks like a zebra!" shouted Henry!

"That is a Zebra Swallowtail butterfly," said Grandpa. "They lay their eggs on pawpaw trees."

"Beside having these butterflies around, why did you decide to grow a pawpaw tree Grandpa?" Henry asked.

"I wanted to grow pawpaws because they are Ohio's native fruit! Native American tribes grew pawpaw trees and even George Washington grew a pawpaw tree on his Mount Vernon estate. And, they are perfect for making ice cream!" Grandpa said.

Henry grabbed a pawpaw from the basket and smelled it. To Henry's surprise it smelled awful! "Why would George Washington like these?" asked Henry as he pinched his nose. "They smell rotten!"

"That's the pawpaw flowers and they smell like that only to attract flies who pollinate them. They taste much better than they smell. Trust me," Grandpa said, "pawpaw is my favorite flavor!"

Eventually, Henry and Grandpa made it back to the house and into the kitchen. "Are you ready to make pawpaw ice cream?" Grandpa asked.

"Ready!" shouted Henry.

Pawpaw Ice Cream

- 2 small pawpaws skin and pits removed
- 1 can coconut milk
- 2 Tbsp maple syrup
- 2 Tbsp lime juice
- Pinch of salt

- mix ingredients together until smooth and place in freezer

Grandpa reached into his pantry and pulled out a recipe card with instructions on how to make pawpaw ice cream. "All we need to do is follow these instructions right here, and we will have ourselves some homemade pawpaw ice cream!" Grandpa said.

So, Henry and Grandpa followed the directions step by step until they had a bowl full of pawpaw ice cream.

Henry scooped up some ice cream and took his first taste. Grandpa was right! Pawpaw was yummy!

"So, do you like it?" asked Grandpa.

"I love it!" Henry said as he scooped another helping of ice cream into his mouth. "I could eat this every day!"

"Well, eating ice cream every day may not be the best thing to do," Grandpa said, "but we can make different food with pawpaws! Next time you visit, we can make pawpaw bread or pawpaw sauce!"

"Could we Grandpa?" Henry asked. "I want to make everything with pawpaws in it! It's my favorite flavor!"

About the Author

Kaitlin Kulich is an Environmental Journalism student at Ohio University who has come to love the natural beauty and unique culture of Southeast Ohio. This is her first children's book and plans to continue writing and working with children throughout her career. Aside from writing, Kaitlin enjoys spending time with family, friends, and day dreaming about her pet pig she plans to have one day.

About the Illustrator

Originally from Cincinnati, Ohio, Laura Dobrota received her BFA from the University of Cincinnati, with a minor in Art Education. Having multiple shows upon graduating, she was also active in teaching art to a wide range of age groups, but primarily within inner city youth. In 2015 she received her MFA in painting and drawing at Ohio University, and continues to reside in the area while regularly exhibiting her art. Laura's desire within her work is to bring an awareness of the natural world, and enjoys exploring how forms occur in nature. In her artistic career she has shown nationally, and internationally, and has participated in many group, solo, invitational, commissioned, and juried exhibitions, and has also received multiple awards and grants. Currently, she is a member of The Art Store in Charleston, West Virginia. She also teaches at Hocking College, and is a member of Starbrick gallery in Nelsonville, Ohio. To learn more about Laura or to contact her, go to her webpage at lauradobrota.weebly.com.